D0576491

Reading Writing and Spelling

Written by Colin Clark
Illustrated by Stephen Holmes

Brown Watson
ENGLAND

Contents

MESSAGE TO PARENTS

This book has been designed to help children in the 5-9 age range to learn and practise their early English language skills. The facts are presented simply and clearly with the use of amusing, colourful illustrations, simple text and numerous games and puzzles. In this way, the book can be used in the home to complement and reinforce the educational process that takes place at school.

Children should be given a work pad to use with this book. Encourage them to write down the answers to all the games and puzzles. In this way they will find it easier to absorb the information. They should not be afraid of making mistakes as they go along. Always remember that learning ought to be an enjoyable experience!

The answers to all the exercises and puzzles can be found at the end of each section.

Reading
and
Writing

MEET THE JONES FAMILY

This is Jack Jones.
Jack is eight years old.

This is Jenny Jones.
Jenny is six years old.

Jenny and Jack live in this house.

4

They live with their mother, Mrs. Jones, their father, Mr. Jones, and their granny, Granny Jones.

The Jones's house is also home to Sniff, the cat, Smelly, the dog and Speedy, the tortoise.

How many people and how many pets are in your home?
Write down all their names on your work pad.
Try and write a sentence to describe each pet.
For example: 'I have a brown dog called Chocolate.'

THE JONES'S HOUSE

There are four bedrooms in the house.
Mr. and Mrs. Jones have a bedroom. It is tidy.

Granny has a bedroom. It is tidy.

Jenny and Jack share a bedroom. It is always in a mess.

The other bedroom is a spare room just now. When Jenny is a little older, she will move out of the bedroom she shares with Jack and move into the spare room. Then Jenny and Jack will each have their own bedrooms and there will be two bedrooms in a mess.

How many bedrooms are there in your house? Write down the names of the people in each bedroom on your work pad.
Write a sentence to describe each bedroom.
For example: 'My little sister's bedroom wall is covered with pictures of pop singers.'

MR. JONES, THE HANDYMAN

Mr. Jones is a hard-working handyman. He is always busy. He does all kinds of work around the house and in the garden.

He paints the inside and outside of houses.

He makes wooden book-shelves and cupboards.

He builds stone walls.

He replaces broken roof tiles.

Are you good at working with your hands?
List the things you can do on your work pad.

Here are four pictures of Mr. Jones at work.

1)

2)

3)

4)

Write a sentence describing what
Mr. Jones is doing in each picture.

MRS. JONES, THE LADY WITH THE TIME TO LISTEN

Mrs. Jones is also a busy person. While her husband is out at work, she works at home. She makes breakfast for the family, then takes the children to school. She makes sure everyone has good food to eat, clean clothes to wear and a clean house to live in. She also has her own computer which she uses to earn money to pay for everything that is needed.

Mrs. Jones works so hard that she often falls asleep in front of the television in the evening. But she is the first one up in the morning and she always has time to listen to anyone who needs to talk to her.

Read the text below. Are the following sentences about Mrs. Jones true or false?

1) The first thing Mrs. Jones does in the morning is take the children to school.
2) Mrs. Jones goes out each day to an office to work on a computer.
3) Mrs. Jones does the cooking and cleaning.
4) Mrs. Jones watches TV in bed in the evening.
5) Mrs. Jones always has time to listen to you.

Is your mum as busy as Mrs. Jones? Write a description of your mum's busy day on your work pad. Show it to your mum and ask her if she thinks your description is accurate.

JACK, JENNY'S BIG BROTHER

Eight-year-old Jack Jones is interested in lots of different things. His favourite subjects at school are English and computer studies. He loves football and wants to be the goalkeeper in the school team when he is older. He is a keen swimmer, particularly good at the butterfly stroke. He likes climbing and often pretends he is a mountaineer. He enjoys his piano lessons and would like to be a famous pianist when he grows up. He often has to look after Jenny, his little sister, but he doesn't mind because they are very good friends.

Answer the following questions on your work pad.

1) What would Jack like to be in the school football team?

2) When Jack goes swimming, which is his favourite stroke?

3) When he is climbing, who does Jack pretend to be?

4) What does Jack want to be when he grows up?

Have you ever been to a musical concert or have you seen one on TV? Write two or three sentences about the music you like or an instrument you play.

JENNY, JACK'S LITTLE SISTER

Jenny is two years younger than Jack. She also likes school, especially English and stories. On Monday mornings, the teacher tells the class a story which she either reads from a book or makes up herself. She then asks the class if anyone would like to tell a story of their own. Jenny loves doing this and has told some wonderful ones. For example, the day she spent as a princess, the time she appeared on television and the occasion when Granny fell off her motorbike!

Jenny's stories would be much better if only she used a greater variety of 'describing words'. Jenny uses the adjective 'nice' far too often. For example, here are a few sentences from her stories. Rewrite them, replacing 'nice' with another adjective from the list below.

1) Nice Jack dived into the water to rescue the nice dog.
2) The nice girl with nice hair was wearing a nice dress.
3) The nice cat ran after the nice mouse.
4) The nice witch turned the nice prince into a frog.
5) The nice sun caused the nice tree to throw a nice shadow.

beautiful	normal	brave	fair	pretty
drowning	lazy	ugly	tabby	bright
handsome	tall	little	flowing	long

GRANNY ON HER MOTORBIKE

Granny Jones is not like other grannies. Other grannies enjoy knitting, shopping, watching TV and drinking cups of tea. Jack and Jenny's granny is very different. She loves to put on her helmet and leather biking suit and ride off into the countryside on her motorbike.

The motorbike used to belong to Grandpa Jones and he and Granny would often go out on it. After Grandpa died, Granny kept the bike for herself. Jack and Jenny can't wait until they are old enough to be allowed to go out with their motorbiking granny!

If you have to tell someone how to get somewhere, you give them directions. For example, you might say: 'Go out of the house and turn left. At the end of the street, turn right. Go to the grocery store, then turn left again...' and so on.

Below is a street map of the town in which the Jones family lives. Granny has to deliver a parcel to a friend's house. Give her clear directions so that she does not take the parcel to the wrong house. Write the directions on your work pad.

Draw a map of the area around your house. Mark the names of the streets, local shops and anything else which might help a friend to find their way.

SNIFF, THE CAT

Sniff is a tabby cat who lives with the Jones family. The children found her one rainy day sitting sadly in a puddle. They brought her home and looked after her. Now Sniff is a large, contented cat. When the weather is good, she likes to stay out all night. If it is cold or wet, Sniff prefers to sleep indoors in her own basket. Sniff likes to settle on people's laps. If they do not move about too much, she begins to purr very loudly. If they do not sit still, Sniff jumps down with a hiss and walks away with her tail swishing.

Sniff hunts the birds in the garden and would love to catch them - but she's too slow! Every time she leaps out of the bushes, the birds fly away and leave Sniff looking mean and disappointed.

Read the story of Sniff carefully, then answer the following questions on your work pad. Please write complete sentences.

1) Where did the children find Sniff?
2) When it rains, where does Sniff sleep?
3) If the person whose lap she is on does not move about, what does Sniff do?
4) What noise does Sniff make when she is angry?
5) Where does Sniff hide when she is hunting birds?

SMELLY, THE DOG

Smelly is a large dog with long, droopy ears whose favourite pastime is chewing bones. When Mrs. Jones gives him a fresh bone, he runs and settles down and chews it for hours on end. Just when the Jones family think he's chewed it to death, Smelly usually sneaks away and buries it. Days, or even weeks later, the bone reappears. It's smelly (that's why he got his name) and horrible, but he chews it again for hours before finally putting it aside for ever.

Sometimes, the bone has been buried in the Jones's garden. However, when they find out the bone is buried in a neighbour's garden, the Jones family have a lot of explaining and apologising to do. Smelly doesn't understand what all the fuss is about.

Smelly has buried his bone somewhere in the Jones's garden. The clues below will help you to find it. Write down on your work pad exactly where the bone is.

The bone is not buried in the grass.
The bone is near some vegetables.
The bone is beside the path.
The bone is near a watering can.
The bone is not in the bushes.
The bone is under a tree.

SPEEDY, THE TORTOISE

The Jones's third pet is a tortoise, called Speedy. He moves around very slowly, eats slowly as well, and particularly enjoys lettuce, cucumber slices and banana. In the summer, Speedy lives in the garden, which is safe because he can't get out of it. He creeps around and spends a lot of time sleeping under bushes. Speedy spends the winter sleeping in a straw-filled hutch in the garage. If he was left out in the cold, he would fall asleep and never wake up. In the warmth of the garage, he wakes up every year when the spring comes.

The sentences opposite tell us about Speedy's busy day. The story does not make sense because the sentences are not in the right order. Rewrite the sentences in the correct order.

Then it was time for another rest, so he plodded back to the bushes. He plodded as fast as he could to the food dish. At daybreak, Speedy woke up. There he found a breakfast of lettuce leaves and banana slices waiting for him. He had had a busy day! In the afternoon, he did it all again. He came out from under the bushes, where he had spent the night. After that, Speedy plodded back to the bushes for a good night's sleep. He walked back to the food dish for his supper.

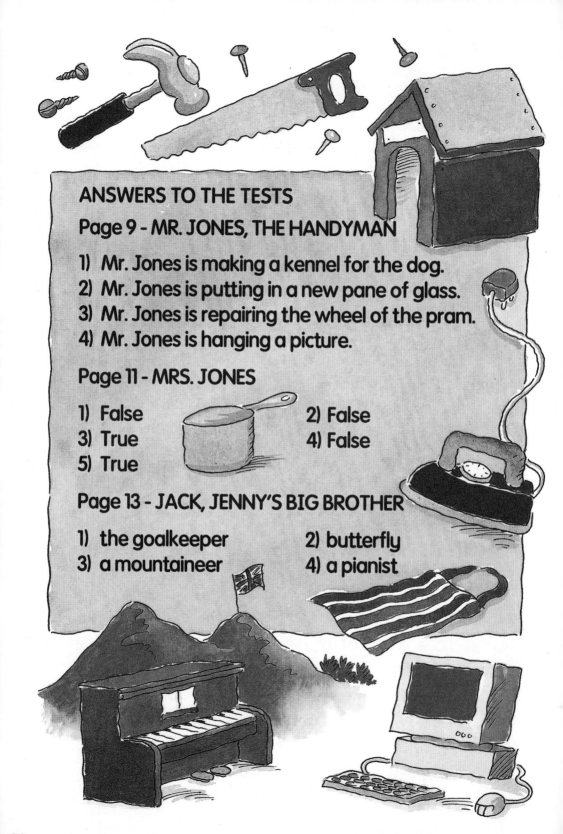

ANSWERS TO THE TESTS

Page 9 - MR. JONES, THE HANDYMAN

1) Mr. Jones is making a kennel for the dog.
2) Mr. Jones is putting in a new pane of glass.
3) Mr. Jones is repairing the wheel of the pram.
4) Mr. Jones is hanging a picture.

Page 11 - MRS. JONES

1) False   2) False
3) True   4) False
5) True

Page 13 - JACK, JENNY'S BIG BROTHER

1) the goalkeeper   2) butterfly
3) a mountaineer   4) a pianist

Page 15 - JENNY, JACK'S LITTLE SISTER

1) Brave Jack dived into the water to rescue the drowning dog.
2) The beautiful girl with fair hair was wearing a pretty dress.
3) The tabby cat ran after the little mouse.
4) The ugly witch turned the handsome prince into a frog.
5) The bright sun caused the tall tree to throw a long shadow.

Page 19 - SNIFF, THE CAT

1) The children found Sniff in a puddle.
2) When it rains, Sniff sleeps in her basket.
3) She begins to purr very loudly.
4) When Sniff is angry she makes a hissing noise.
5) Sniff hides in the bushes.

Page 21 - SMELLY, THE DOG

Smelly has buried his bone right in the middle of the picture, at the side of the path, under the tree.

Page 22-23 - SPEEDY, THE TORTOISE

At daybreak, Speedy woke up. He came out from under the bushes, where he had spent the night. He plodded as fast as he could to the food dish. There he found a breakfast of lettuce leaves and banana slices waiting for him. Then it was time for another rest, so he plodded back to the bushes. In the afternoon, he did it all again. He walked back to the food dish for his supper. After that, Speedy plodded back to the bushes for a good night's sleep. He had had a busy day!

Spelling

THE ALPHABET

Name each of the following objects pictured below. Each one begins with a different letter of the alphabet. To help you, we have put in the first letter of each word in alphabetical order. We have also put in a dash for each missing letter. Write the words on your work pad.

1) a _ _

2) b _ _

3) c _ _

4) d _ _

5) e _ _

6) f _ _ _

7) g _ _ _

8) h _ _

9) i _ _

10) j _ _

11) k _ _

12) l _ _ _

13) m _ _ _ _

14) n _ _ _

15) o _ _

16) p _ _

17) q _ _ _ _ _

18) r _ _ _

19) s _ _ _ _

20) t _ _ _

21) u _ _ _ _ _ _ _

22) v _ _ _ _ _

23) w _ _ _ _

24) x _ _ _ _ _ _ _

25) y _ _ _ _

26) z _ _ _ _

WORDS BEGINNING WITH d

There are 10 things in the picture below which begin with the letter **d**. Can you find them all? Write the answers on your work pad.

ANIMAL NAMES ENDING WITH **t**

There are 10 animals shown below with names ending with the letter **t**. Can you spot them? Write the answers on your work pad.

MAKE YOUR OWN WORDS

The following letters of the alphabet are known as consonants:

b c d f g h j k l m n
p q r s t v w x y z

Words often begin with two of these consonants put together in a 'blend'. We have listed some of these blends below. Choose a blend to complete each of the words pictured and write the completed words on your work pad.

st cl dr gr pl tr sc

_ _ ar   _ _ ee   _ _ ug

_ _ um   _ _ agon   _ _ arf

__eps

__ass

__ock

__ant

__oud

__ain

__apes

__ip

__ones

__iff

__ales

__unk

__ay

__um

__amp

33

THE DIFFERENCE AN **e** MAKES

At the end of many words, when an **e** is added or taken away, we get a new word that sounds quite different to the original one.

Try adding an **e** to the words printed on this page to make new words that go with the pictures. Say both the old words and the new ones and write them down side by side on your work pad.

can

pip

fir

kit

man

not

pan

win

bar

Now take away the **e** at the end of the words on this page and write the new words on your work pad.

care

mate

tape

huge

fine

tripe

dame

plane

scare

plume

cape

hate

LOOKS THE SAME, SOUNDS DIFFERENT

These letters of the alphabet are known as vowels:

a   e   i   o   u

Lots of words contain two vowels side by side, but sometimes the same two vowels together can make more than one sound.

ea has two sounds: as in st**ea**l and inst**ea**d.

Write the words **steal** and **instead** on your work pad. Then, under **steal**, list the words pictured below which sound like **steal** when you say them. Write down under **instead**, all the words which sound like this when you say them.

br _ _ d   h _ _ d   t _ _

st _ _ m   p _ _ ch   thr _ _ d

36

Sometimes, when a vowel and a consonant are in combination, we also find that they look the same but have different sounds.

ow has two sounds: as in s**low** and n**ow**.

Write the words **slow** and **now** on your work pad. Then, under **slow**, list the words pictured here which sound like **slow** when you say them. Write down under **now**, all the words which sound like this word when you say them.

s n _ _

b l _ _

c r _ _

c _ _

c r _ _ n

c l _ n

m _ _

_ _ l

t _ _ e r

LOOKS DIFFERENT, SOUNDS THE SAME

Sometimes letter combinations look different but sound exactly the same when we say them.

oy and **oi** make the same sound: as in b**oy** and b**oi**l.

Write the words **boy** and **boil** on your work pad. List underneath them all the words pictured below which have the combination **oy** or **oi** in them.

p _ _ nt

c _ _ l

t _ _

_ _ l

c _ _ n

j _ _

h _ _ st

cowb _ _

j _ _ nt

ay and **ai** make the same sound: as in **pay** and **paint**.

Write the words **pay** and **paint** on your word pad and list underneath them all the words pictured below which have the combination **ay** or **ai** in them.

r _ _ n

displ _ _

p _ _ nter

r _ _

pr _ _

s _ _ l

sn _ _ l

compl _ _ n

tr _ _ n

WORDS IN TWO PARTS

Some words are made up of two shorter words joined together.

Here is an example.

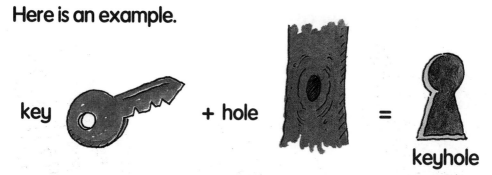

key + hole = keyhole

There are four picture sums like this shown below. Each sum shows pictures of two small words that together make up a longer, two-part word. Write down the answer to each picture sum on your work pad.

ANIMAL WORD SQUARE

The names of 13 different animals are hidden in this word square. Find their names and write them on your work pad. We have pictured some of the animals around the square. Take care! Not all the animals pictured are in the word square!

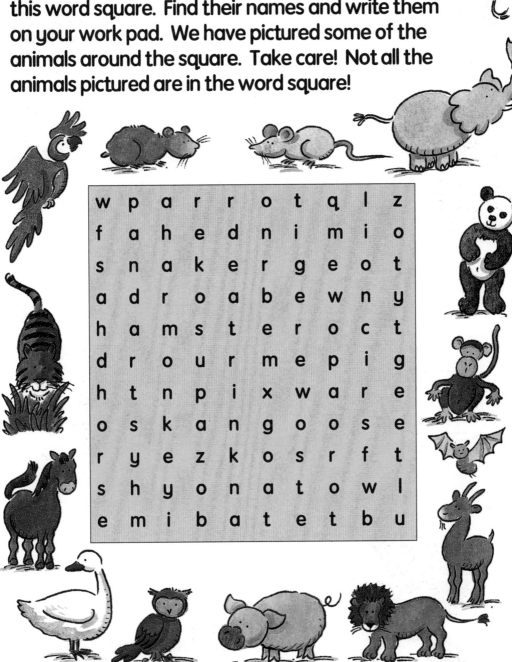

w	p	a	r	r	o	t	q	l	z
f	a	h	e	d	n	i	m	i	o
s	n	a	k	e	r	g	e	o	t
a	d	r	o	a	b	e	w	n	y
h	a	m	s	t	e	r	o	c	t
d	r	o	u	r	m	e	p	i	g
h	t	n	p	i	x	w	a	r	e
o	s	k	a	n	g	o	o	s	e
r	y	e	z	k	o	s	r	f	t
s	h	y	o	n	a	t	o	w	l
e	m	i	b	a	t	e	t	b	u

Pages 28-29 THE ALPHABET

1) ant   2) boy   3) cat
4) dog   5) egg   6) fire
7) girl   8) hat   9) ice
10) jar   11) key   12) leaf
13) mouse   14) nest   15) oar
16) pig   17) quilt   18) rose
19) smoke   20) tree   21) umbrella
22) violin   23) watch   24) xylophone
25) yacht   26) zebra

Page 30 - WORDS BEGINNING WITH d

duck, doll, dinosaur, door, dartboard, darts, drum, desk, dog, drawing

Page 31 - ANIMAL NAMES ENDING WITH t

bat, parrot, rabbit, cat, rat, goat, newt, elephant, ant, piglet

Page 32-33 - MAKE YOUR OWN WORDS

star, tree, plug,
drum, dragon, scarf
steps, grass, clock,
plant, cloud, grain,
grapes, drip, scones,
cliff, scales, trunk,
tray, plum, stamp

Pages 34-35 - THE DIFFERENCE AN **e** MAKES

cane, pipe, fire,
kite, mane, note,
pane, wine, bare

car, mat, tap,
hug, fin, trip
dam, plan, scar,
plum, cap, hat

Page 36 - LOOKS THE SAME,
   SOUNDS DIFFERENT

instead
bread, head, thread
steal
tea, steam, peach

Page 37

slow
snow, blow, crow, mow
now
cow, crown, clown, owl, tower

Page 38 - LOOKS DIFFERENT, SOUNDS THE SAME

boy
toy, joy, cowboy
boil
point, oil, coin, coil, joint, hoist

Page 39

pay
ray, pray, display
paint
rain, snail, train, complain, sail, painter

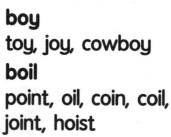

Page 40 - WORDS IN TWO PARTS

cowboy, pancake, eggcup, treehouse

Page 41 - ANIMAL WORD SQUARE

parrot, panda, snake, tiger, lion, hamster, pig, monkey, goose, horse, bat, goat, owl

Punctuation

WHY DO WE HAVE PUNCTUATION?

Here are the first few lines of the famous story by Lewis Carroll, Alice in Wonderland. They have been printed without any punctuation. See if you can make any sense of them.

Alice was beginning to get very tired of sitting by her sister on the bank and of having nothing to do once or twice she had peeped into the book her sister was reading but it had no pictures or conversations in it and what is the use of a book thought Alice without pictures or conversation

It is not easy to read this, is it?

Now try reading it again with punctuation.

Alice was beginning to get very tired of sitting by her sister, and of having nothing to do: once or twice she had peeped into the book her sister was reading, but it had no pictures or conversations in it, "and what is the use of a book," thought Alice, "without pictures or conversation?"

It is easier to read with punctuation, isn't it?

WHAT DO PUNCTUATION MARKS MEAN?

There are eleven punctuation marks that we use in written English. These are:-

full stop	**.**	The bells are ringing.
question mark	**?**	Why are the bells ringing?
exclamation mark	**!**	What a noise the bells make!
comma	**,**	The bells are ringing, because there is a wedding.
hyphen	**—**	The bell-ringers are tired.

dash	—	The bells are ringing – but the old dog does not hear them.
brackets	( )	The bells (all four of them) are ringing.
colon	:	All four bell-ringers are ready: Mr. and Mrs. Brown and the twins.
semi-colon	;	There is something wrong; one of the bells is cracked.
inverted commas	" "	"I hate the bells," says Granny.
apostrophe	'	The bells are so loud; it's not Granny's fault she hates them.

FULL STOP

Just as every sentence must begin with a capital letter, so a full stop is the usual punctuation mark which shows that a sentence has ended. It is the punctuation mark that we use most often at the end of sentences.

The following words do not make sense unless we put a full stop at the end of each sentence.

My name is Katie I am seven years old I live in the country my Mum and Dad have a farm

My name is Katie. I am seven years old. I live in the country. My Mum and Dad have a farm.

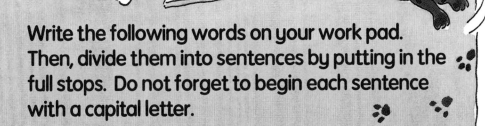

Write the following words on your work pad. Then, divide them into sentences by putting in the full stops. Do not forget to begin each sentence with a capital letter.

You should see the mess in my bedroom the cat climbed in the window while I was out now my bed is covered in mud

In the following sentences, the full stops are in the wrong places. Write the sentences with the full stops where they ought to be. Don't forget the capital letters!

Jill had to do something. To save her dog the witch had almost dragged Scruffy. Out of the house Jill picked up the soup spoon and gave the witch a crack. On the knuckles the witch screamed and let go of Scruffy.

QUESTION MARK

At the end of a sentence that asks a question, we put in a question mark. When we are talking, the way we say something tells the other person we are asking a question. When we are writing, we must put in the question mark.

Copy these sentences on to your pad and put a full stop or a question mark at the end of each one.

Where is my biscuit

Someone has eaten your biscuit

Who has eaten it

Did the dog eat it

It looks like it

Look at the picture above. Write down the answers to the questions on your work pad.

1) How many mice can you see?

2) What is one of the mice eating?

3) Where are the other mice hiding?

4) What are the other mice looking at?

5) What is the old mouse holding?

EXCLAMATION MARK

An exclamation mark can be used instead of a full stop at the end of a sentence. It can also be used even after just a word or two, to express emotion. For example:

Look at that!
The horse has eaten my hat.

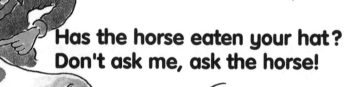

Has the horse eaten your hat?
Don't ask me, ask the horse!

Help! The horse has eaten my hat.

Write the following on your work pad. Put either an exclamation mark or a question mark at the end of each one.

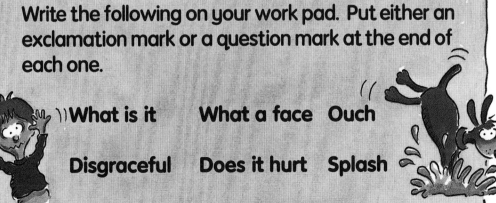

What is it   What a face   Ouch

Disgraceful   Does it hurt   Splash

COMMA

Very often, to make the sense clearer, it is necessary to have a brief pause, or a number of brief pauses, in a sentence. The most common punctuation mark used for these brief pauses is the comma.

For example, it is much easier to read and understand the sentence on the right than the one on the left.

To get to the pet shop turn left then second right then go straight on to the next corner where you will see it.

To get to the pet shop, turn left, then second right, then go straight on to the next corner, where you will see it.

We also put a comma after names in a list, instead of using the word **and** all the time. The second sentence sounds better, doesn't it?

Hilary and Hannah and Hilda have put on their best hats because they are going to a party.

Hilary, Hannah and Hilda have put on their best hats, because they are going to a party.

Copy the following sentences on to your work pad, putting in commas where they are needed.

Big or small young or old crocodiles love to sleep in the sun.

If you are too tired you will not be able to stay awake.

John is the son of Bill the best baker in town.

HYPHEN

A hyphen is used to join two words together to become what is called a compound word. For example, the words **well** and **known** are joined together with a hyphen to become **well-known**.

Each of the words in the first line below can be joined with a hyphen to one of the words in the second line to make a compound word. Write all five compound words on your work pad.

twenty	lay	half	right	big
by	term	handed	headed	two

man eating lion   man-eating lion

DASH

A dash is used when a sentence suddenly changes direction.

Dad put on his hat and coat and went out – but he had forgotten to put his trousers on!

Katie's painting of a kite – a very colourful affair – was soon stuck on the wall in her bedroom.

BRACKETS

Brackets can be used instead of dashes before and after a secondary thought in a sentence. Brackets must always be used in pairs. There must be an opening bracket at the beginning and a closing bracket at the end of the secondary thought or extra piece of information.

The children took some books to read (and plenty to eat) on their coach trip to the sea.

The little country mouse gave all that she had (one nut) to the hungry town mouse.

A name in brackets can also make it clear who it is we are referring to in a sentence.

The teacher told John that he (the teacher) had not always done his homework when he was young.

Write the following sentences on your work pad, replacing dashes with brackets where you think it is right to do so.

The girl took off her gloves and her coat – but she kept her hat on.

Fred was a friendly dog – he wanted to lick everyone – but was too big to keep indoors.

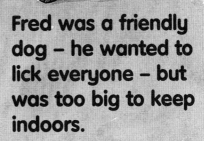

Abigail was a beautiful cat – a real Persian – and she was very fussy about her appearance.

COLON

We use a colon immediately before we make a list of some kind or before a quotation.

Aunt Agatha brought everything with her: luggage, handbag, shopping bag, umbrella, cat basket and cat.

Young Percy would often quote Shakespeare: 'Friends, Romans, countrymen, lend me your ears!'

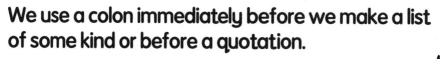

Write the following sentences on your work pad, putting in a colon each time, if you think the sentence needs one.

Morris had three pictures, a pretty mouse, a piece of cheese and the house cat.

The manager addressed the football team, 'On the one hand, you have played with great spirit, on the other, we have lost every game.'

SEMI-COLON

A semi-colon is the punctuation mark for a longer pause than that marked by a comma. A semi-colon is used to join two parts of a long sentence. It is used instead of words like **and, but** and **because**.

Wilf was not allowed to play football that day; he had left one boot at home.

The other animals did not like it when Hattie came to tea; she broke all their chairs.

Write these sentences on your work pad, putting in a semi-colon where one is needed.

Bill and Ben are two gorillas – Bill is bigger.

Sally tripped over the rug and fell on the cat, Sally's dinner fell on Granny.

INVERTED COMMAS

Inverted commas are used to mark the beginning and end of speech. Sometimes there are two inverted commas and sometimes only one.

> **"How are you, Your Highness?" asked Tom.**
> **"I am very well," replied the princess.**
> **The king said: "I feel terrible."**
> **"I am so sorry, Your Majesty," said Tom.**

Remember that all the spoken sentence, including the full stop, question mark or exclamation mark at the end, goes inside the inverted commas.

Sometimes it is necessary to break a spoken sentence into two parts. Then you must always remember to begin and end each part of the sentence with inverted commas. No capital letter is needed at the start of the second half of the sentence.

If the spoken sentence is only reported and the actual words are not used, no inverted commas are required.

"I have a headache," the king told Tom.

The king told Tom that he had a headache.

APOSTROPHE

An apostrophe is used to show that something belongs to someone. The apostrophe is put after the owner and followed by an **s**.

Here is Joe.
Here is a book.
It is Joe's book.

When there are two or more owners, the apostrophe comes after the **s**.

The socks belong to the boys.
They are the boys' socks.

When there are two or more owners and the word does not end in **s** (eg. men, children), the apostrophe is followed by an **s**.

The toys belong to the children.
They are the children's toys.

Some belonging words which end in **s** are called pronouns. They are possessive themselves and do not need an apostrophe.

his   her   its
ours   yours   theirs

Is that football **yours**?
No, that is the teacher's football.
It is **his**.

The other use of the apostrophe is to show that a letter, or some letters, have been left out of a word.

isn't = is not (the letter **o** has been left out)

I've = I have (the letters **ha** have been left out)

Other examples of words that use the apostrophe are:
    who's = who is,   I'll = I will,   can't = cannot
    he's = he is,   it's = it is,   who'd = who would

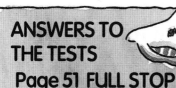

ANSWERS TO THE TESTS

Page 51 FULL STOP

You should see the mess in my bedroom. The cat climbed in the window while I was out. Now my bed is covered in mud.

Jill had to do something to save her dog. The witch had almost dragged Scruffy out of the house. Jill picked up the soup spoon and gave the witch a crack on the knuckles. The witch screamed and let go of Scruffy.

Page 52-53 QUESTION MARK

Where is my biscuit?
Someone has eaten your biscuit.
Who has eaten it?
Did the dog eat it?
It looks like it.

1) Four mice.
2) Some cheese.
3) Behind the loaf of bread.
4) The cat.
5) A walking stick.

Page 55 EXCLAMATION MARK

What is it?	What a face!	Ouch!
Disgraceful!	Does it hurt?	Splash!

Page 57 COMMA

Big or small, young or old, crocodiles love to sleep in the sun.

If you are too tired, you will not be able to stay awake.

John is the son of Bill, the best baker in town.

Page 58 HYPHEN

twenty-two   lay-by   half-term

right-handed   big-headed

Page 61 BRACKETS

The girl took off her gloves and her coat — but she kept her hat on.

Fred was a friendly dog (he wanted to lick everyone), but was too big to keep indoors.

Abigail was a beautiful cat (a real Persian) and she was very fussy about her appearance.

Page 62 COLON

Morris had three pictures: a pretty mouse, a piece of cheese and the house cat.

The manager addressed the football team: 'On the one hand, you have played with great spirit, on the other, we have lost every game.'

Page 63 SEMI-COLON

Bill and Ben are two gorillas; Bill is bigger.

Sally tripped over the rug and fell on the cat; Sally's dinner fell on Granny.

Grammar

WHAT IS A SENTENCE?

A sentence is usually a group of words which makes sense by itself. A sentence must start with a capital letter and end with either a full stop, a question mark or an exclamation mark. Each of the following is a sentence.

Katie has a dirty face.

Isn't Katie's face dirty?

What a dirty face Katie has!

Sometimes a sentence can be just two words.

Come here!   Go away!   Get washed!

Sort out these mixed up sentences and write them down correctly on your work pad.

on the fence. The elephant is sitting
pulling Sally's hair. The monkey is
the cake. is eating The mouse

Use the words below to write proper sentences on your work pad. Begin with a capital letter and finish with a full stop, question mark or exclamation mark.

like chocolate do you

out get

much how the apples are

rough sea the today is

VERBS

A verb is the 'doing word' in a sentence — the word that tells us what a person or thing is doing or what is happening to them.

A woodpecker **pecks** on wood.
The truck is **tipping** sand out
of the back.

Pick a verb out of this list to complete each sentence and write the completed sentences on your work pad.

combs   watches
find   carry

Rapunzel _____ her long hair.

It is difficult to _____ all the boxes.

The detective hopes to _____ a clue.

Our cat _____ television all the time.

These sentences have the wrong verb in them.
Choose the correct verb and write each sentence
on your work pad.

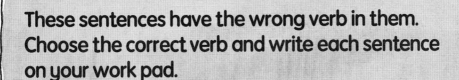

We pour a lemon.   We squeeze our shoes.

We light a knot.   We tie the fire.

We polish the orange juice.

Pick the correct verb for each sentence and write it
on your work pad.

a) I (cook/clean/paint) my teeth after a meal.
b) The hen has just (cooked/buried/laid) an egg.
c) Please (burn/wash/shake) the plates for me.

THE SUBJECT

The subject of a sentence is the word or words identifying the person, place or thing doing an action. This word can be a noun, a proper noun or a pronoun.

Nouns are the words used for naming things. Names which refer to a person, place or thing individually are called proper nouns and always begin with a capital letter.

Some nouns

for a person	–	teacher	nurse	girl
for a place	–	house	kennel	palace
for a thing	–	egg	pencil	torch

Some proper nouns

for a person	–	Tom	Katie	Queen
for a place	–	London	France	Parliament
for a thing	–	Bible	Easter	Concorde

Pronouns are words used instead of nouns. These are the pronouns which we use as subjects:

I   you   he   she   it   we   they

Mary saw Simon pulling faces.
She saw Simon pulling faces.

Mary is the subject of both sentences, but in the second sentence, the pronoun **she** is used instead of Mary.

Can you pick the correct subject for each sentence? Write the sentences on your work pad.

The doctor   Mary   He   The kennel

_____ fell over the football.

_____ was too small for the dog.

_____ put a bandage on Paul's knee.

_____ put on a lovely dress.

THE OBJECT

The object of a sentence is the person, place or thing to which the subject is doing something. The word or words for the object can be a noun, a proper noun or a pronoun.

As in the case of the subject, pronouns are words used instead of nouns. These are the pronouns we use as objects.

me   you   him   her   it   us   them

Ann helped John to wash the dog.
Ann helped him to wash the dog.

John is the object of both sentences, but in the second sentence, the pronoun **him** is used instead of John.

For each of these sentences, write down on your word pad:
a) the subject
b) the object

1) The elephant is wearing a hat.
2) The fairy flapped her wings.
3) Snakes do not have legs.
4) Henry loves ice cream.

Look at the sentences below. Rewrite the second sentence replacing the underlined words with pronouns.

1) Cindy has a new coat. <u>The coat</u> cost <u>Cindy</u> a lot of money.

2) The children had a box of chocolates. <u>The children</u> ate <u>the chocolates</u>.

3) Granny has two cats. <u>Granny</u> lets <u>the cats</u> sleep on her bed.

ADJECTIVES

Adjectives tell us more about nouns. They are 'describing words'.

Here are some nouns. Pick an adjective from those listed below to describe each noun.

1) forest   2) scream   3) game
4) town   5) flower   6) load

yellow   heavy   clever   loud   thick
wooden   quiet   sticky   close   bold

Pick out the adjectives in the following sentences. Write the adjectives on your word pad.

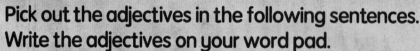

1) Rex is a friendly, little puppy.
2) The shiny aircraft made a roaring noise.
3) The haunted house is in the dark woods.
4) The new teacher had long hair and wore a battered, old hat.
5) Susan had muddy shoes and a torn dress.

Choose the right adjectives from the selection below to complete the following sentences. List your chosen words on your work pad.

1) The _____ cat sat on Mum's hat.
2) _____ sharks try to catch fish in their _____ mouths.
3) _____ Peter had _____ problems with _____ sums.
4) The _____ pot gave off a _____ smell.

ginger	steaming	huge	weeping
difficult	fierce	poor	serious
smiling	truly	best	horrible

Below are ten balloons. Each one has half a word on it. Join the halves together and write the five adjectives on your work pad.

bro   squ   flu   yel   lly
sme   ken   are   ffy   low

ADVERBS

An adverb does for a verb what an adjective does for a noun; an adverb adds more meaning to a verb.

Some adverbs are spelt the same whether they are used as an adjective or as an adverb. For example:

Fred was on the early train. (early as an adjective, describing the train)

Fred's train arrived early. (early as an adverb, adding meaning to the verb **arrived**)

Some adjectives become adverbs simply by adding **ly** to the end of the word. Others have to change spelling to become adverbs.

sweet – sweetly   poor – poorly   rare – rarely
happy – happily   gentle – gently   speedy – speedily

Make adverbs from all the adjectives listed here and write the words on your work pad.

regular   precise   wealthy   powerful
heavy   glad   hungry   noisy

Choose the right adverb for each of these sentences. Write them on your work pad.

politely   bravely   beautifully   greedily

1) _____ , he gave up his seat for the old lady.

3) The children _____ went to the cat's rescue.

4) The pigs ate their food _____ .

2) She danced _____ that evening.

PREPOSITIONS

Prepositions are words which are used to tell us where or how someone or something stands in relation to another person or thing. Most prepositions are short words, but some consist of groups of words.

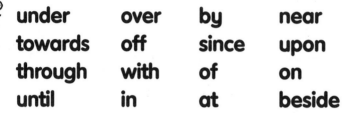

Here are some prepositions:-

under	over	by	near
towards	off	since	upon
through	with	of	on
until	in	at	beside

in spite of   as soon as   because of   except for

Find the preposition in each of these sentences. Write your answers on your work pad.

1) The mouse was sitting beside the cheese.
2) The mouse ran away as soon as the cat appeared.
3) The cat ran along the wall.
4) The dog was tied to the gatepost.

Sometimes, two prepositions are used together.

Bob jumped **down from** the wall.
Bess did not come **until after** we had finished lunch.

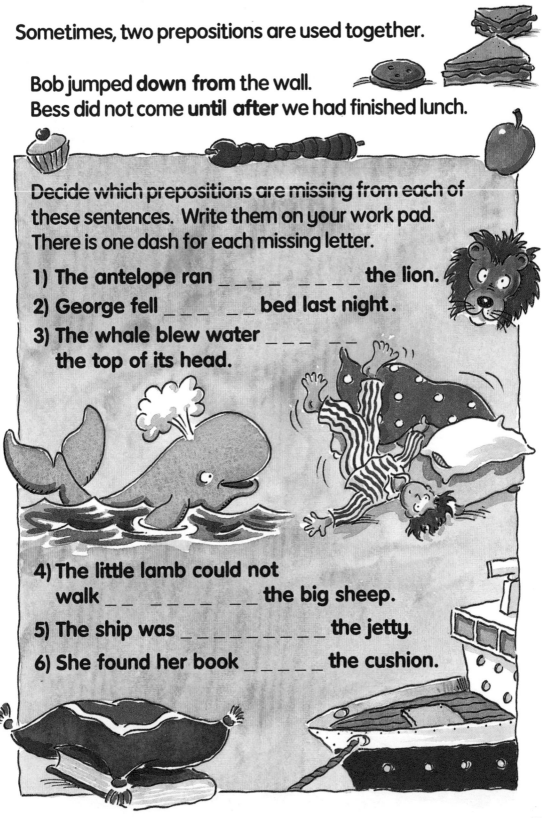

Decide which prepositions are missing from each of
these sentences. Write them on your work pad.
There is one dash for each missing letter.

1) The antelope ran _ _ _ _ _ _ _ _ the lion.
2) George fell _ _ _ _ _ bed last night.
3) The whale blew water _ _ _ _ _
   the top of its head.

4) The little lamb could not
   walk _ _ _ _ _ _ _ _ the big sheep.
5) The ship was _ _ _ _ _ _ _ _ _ _ the jetty.
6) She found her book _ _ _ _ _ _ the cushion.

CONJUNCTIONS

Conjunctions are words used to join one thought to another thought. They join groups of words together, showing in what relation one group stands to the other.

Conjunctions are usually single words, like:-

and   but   if   because   before   after   when   until

but sometimes they can be two words, like:-

either – or,   both – and,   whether – or,   even – if

Find the conjunctions in each of these sentences. Write your answers on your work pad.

1. Daniel is a talented and hard-working player.
2. Nobody likes Sharon because she is so bad-tempered.
3. Either that dog leaves this house or I do.

Conjunctions come before a reason, as in:

Billy drank a lot of water, because he was thirsty.

Conjunctions can show time, as in:

She has stopped riding her bike, since she last fell off.

Conjunctions can show the result of something, as in:

He did not do his homework, therefore the teacher kept him in after school.

The conjunctions are missing from these sentences. Write them on your work pad.

1) **The monkey climbed the tree easily,_____ the elephant could not get off the ground.**

2) **_____ its size, the crocodile is a good swimmer.**

3) **Fred opened the door _____ entered the house.**

SIMPLE SENTENCES

A simple sentence is one that has only one verb, which describes only one thing or idea.

The following are all simple sentences.

**Kevin likes books.
A kennel is a little house for a dog.
The girls are playing netball.**

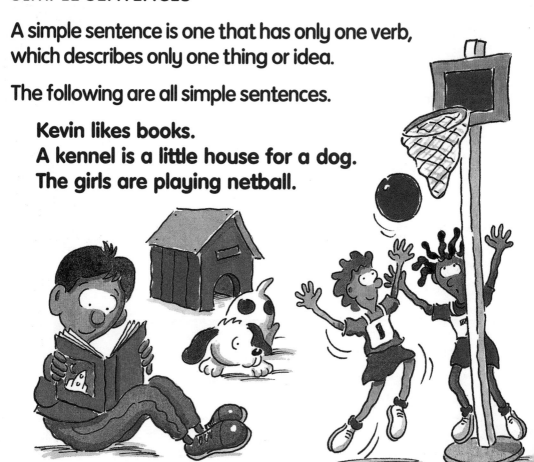

DOUBLE SENTENCES

A double sentence is made up of two parts joined by a conjunction. In the following example, two separate sentences have been joined up by the word **and**, making one double sentence.

Eddie rang the bell. The door opened at once.

Eddie rang the bell and the door opened at once.

COMPLEX SENTENCES

A complex sentence has more than one verb in it and describes more than one thing or idea.

Here are some complex sentences.

The fox is very fond of hounds that can't smell.

Sophie has a new dress that fits her very well.

Sometimes, Susie wears a dress that belongs to her sister.

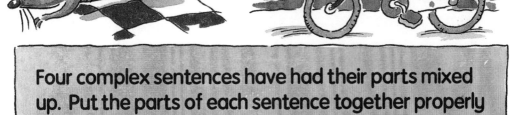

Four complex sentences have had their parts mixed up. Put the parts of each sentence together properly and write the answers on your work pad.

Polly is riding a bike that barks all night.

Mum hates any mouse that she is very proud of.

The cat has a new kitten that belongs to Ian.

Arthur complains about the dog that comes into the kitchen.

VERBS: PRESENT AND PAST TENSE

When a verb tells us about something that is happening at this moment, we say that it is in the **present tense**.

    Present tense   **Mary washes her hair.**

When the verb tells us about something that happened before now (in the past), we say it is in the **past tense**.

    Past tense   **Mary washed her hair.**

The sentences below are in the present tense. Write them in the past tense, telling us what happened yesterday.

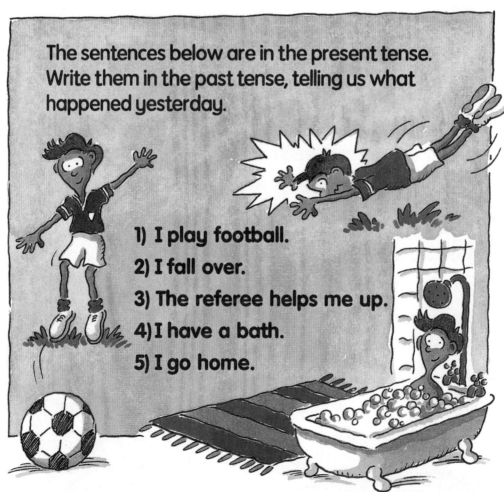

1) I play football.
2) I fall over.
3) The referee helps me up.
4) I have a bath.
5) I go home.

ONE AND MORE THAN ONE

When a noun refers to one person, object or idea, it is **singular**.

When a noun refers to more than one person, object or idea, it is **plural**.

These nouns are **singular**:

    apple shoe egg girl hand thought

These nouns are **plural**:

    apples shoes eggs girls hands thoughts

The general rule for forming the plural of a noun is to add an **s** at the end.

One **snake** becomes two **snakes**.
One **skyscraper** becomes two **skyscrapers**.

If a word ends with **s**, **ss**, **sh**, **ch**, or **x**, we must add **es** to the end of the word to make it plural.

s one atlas — two atlases
ss one glass — two glasses
sh one dash   — two dashes
ch one bench — two benches
x one box   — two boxes

Write the following words in the plural.

map   stone   house
tax   coach   bunch
brush   wall   address
colour   letter   powder

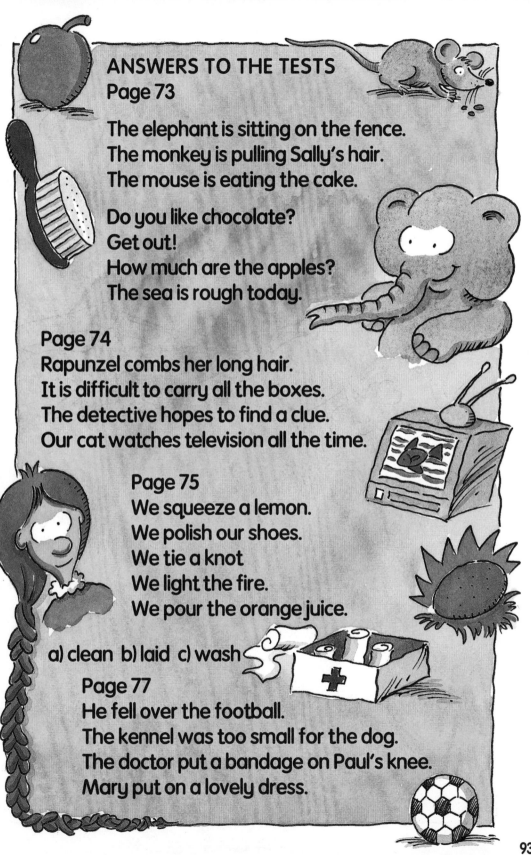

ANSWERS TO THE TESTS
Page 73

The elephant is sitting on the fence.
The monkey is pulling Sally's hair.
The mouse is eating the cake.

Do you like chocolate?
Get out!
How much are the apples?
The sea is rough today.

Page 74
Rapunzel combs her long hair.
It is difficult to carry all the boxes.
The detective hopes to find a clue.
Our cat watches television all the time.

Page 75
We squeeze a lemon.
We polish our shoes.
We tie a knot
We light the fire.
We pour the orange juice.

a) clean b) laid c) wash

Page 77
He fell over the football.
The kennel was too small for the dog.
The doctor put a bandage on Paul's knee.
Mary put on a lovely dress.

Page 79

1) subject – The elephant   object – a hat
2) subject – The fairy   object – her wings
3) subject – Snakes   object – legs
4) subject – Henry   object – ice cream

1) It cost her a lot of money.
2) They ate them.
3) She lets them sleep on her bed.

Page 80

1) thick 2) loud 3) close 4) quiet 5) yellow 6) heavy

1) friendly little 2) shiny roaring
3) haunted dark 4) new long battered old
5) muddy torn

Page 81

1) ginger 2) Fierce huge 3) Poor serious difficult
4) steaming horrible

bro-ken squ-are flu-ffy yel-low sme-lly

Page 83

regularly   precisely   wealthily   powerfully
heavily   gladly   hungrily   noisily

1) Politely 2) bravely 3) greedily 4) beautifully

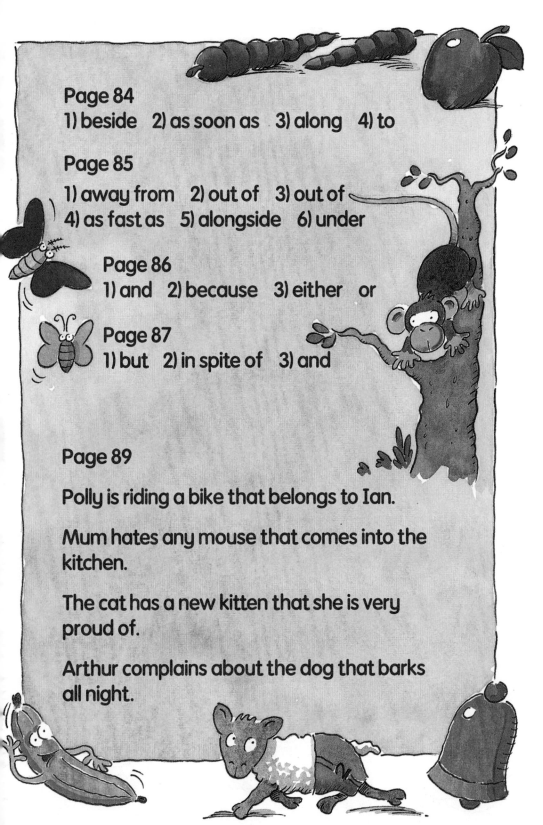

Page 84
1) beside   2) as soon as   3) along   4) to

Page 85
1) away from   2) out of   3) out of
4) as fast as   5) alongside   6) under

Page 86
1) and   2) because   3) either   or

Page 87
1) but   2) in spite of   3) and

Page 89

Polly is riding a bike that belongs to Ian.

Mum hates any mouse that comes into the kitchen.

The cat has a new kitten that she is very proud of.

Arthur complains about the dog that barks all night.

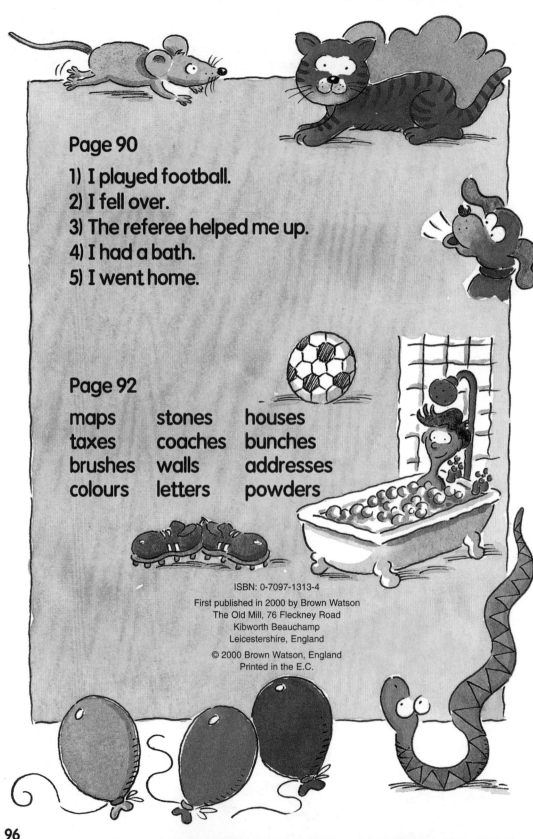

Page 90

1) I played football.
2) I fell over.
3) The referee helped me up.
4) I had a bath.
5) I went home.

Page 92

maps	stones	houses
taxes	coaches	bunches
brushes	walls	addresses
colours	letters	powders

ISBN: 0-7097-1313-4

First published in 2000 by Brown Watson
The Old Mill, 76 Fleckney Road
Kibworth Beauchamp
Leicestershire, England

© 2000 Brown Watson, England
Printed in the E.C.